GRANDMA GUMMY'S GARDEN

Written by Shawn Wesner • Illustrated by Devin Wineinger

Grandma Gummy's Garden

Written by Shawn Wesner
Illustrated by Devin Wineinger
Page Design by Kerrice Mapes

ISBN: 979-8-9911560-6-6

Wakarusa, KS
personalchapterspublishing.com

This story is dedicated to all the Grandparents
who impart their wisdom and experiences upon those they love.

*Thank you to my children Addison, Joaquin and Teagan
who influenced this story and my life.*

When I was a little girl, I lived in Southern Africa. Every summer I would visit America and for one week I would stay with my Grandma Gummy.

The name Grandma Gummy was given by my sister, Addison. When we were young, we came to expect a piece of gum from Grandma every time we visited.

During those summers, Grandma Gummy and I would spend time in her garden. We would pick tomatoes and peppers and other vegetables.

ne day I asked her why she likes to garden and she said, "because it is peaceful."

I didn't understand what that meant, so she explained to me peaceful means you don't have to worry about things.

~   I don't like to worry, so that sounded nice.

My grandma taught me a lot during those visits; not only about gardening but also about her life.

I learned she loves to travel, cook, sew and cut hair.

But the thing she loves the most is her .

My grandma had a very special friend named Kay. Grandma Gummy and Kay had a lot in common.

Like my grandma, Kay also loved to travel. She traveled all over the world and would bring gifts home from her adventures.

Grandma and Kay had something else in common. They both had a strong sense of community.

I didn't understand what was meant by that.

Grandma told me the people who live near you make up your community. She said when you can, you should do nice things for people in your community who aren't as fortunate as you.

"How do you do that?"
I asked.

She said, "You can
grow vegetables in your
garden and give them
to people who can't
afford them, or you can
volunteer your time."

"What does volunteer mean?" I asked.

"It is when you give your time to others so you both can feel happy."

I like it when people are **happy**.

Grandma told me that Kay built a garden in her community for people to visit to feel peaceful and happy.

I thought that sounded like a nice thing to do.

If you want to feel peaceful and happy, you can visit this garden too. You don't have to live in Topeka to experience Kay's Garden. You can visit it online at: *TopekaZoo.org/kay-mcfarland-japanese-garden/*

Kay's Garden

Grandma Gummy also said it's important for grandparents to teach their children and grandchildren what makes them happy. That way they can learn important lessons about their life story.

"What if people don't have a garden to visit to learn these lessons?" I asked.

Grandma Gummy said they can write their life story.

I thought that sounded hard.

Grandma said it's not; it's actually easy to do. Her friend Kay made sure of this.

"How do you do that?" I asked.

She said there is a website where anyone can share their story, free of charge. Again, thanks to her friend, Kay.

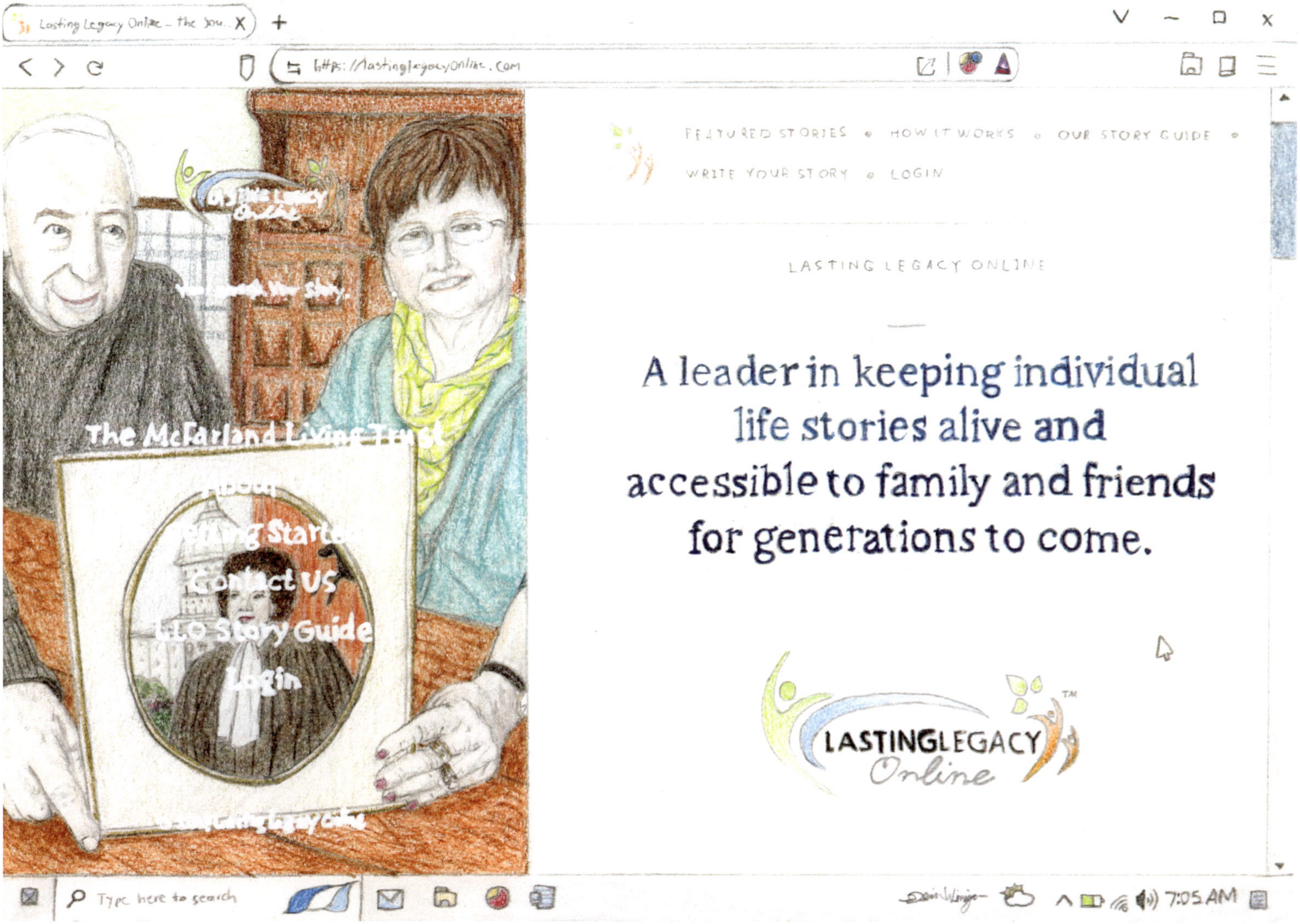

FEATURED STORIES • HOW IT WORKS • OUR STORY GUIDE •

WRITE YOUR STORY • LOGIN

LASTING LEGACY ONLINE

A leader in keeping individual
life stories alive and
accessible to family and friends
for generations to come.

LASTING LEGACY
Online
™

The McFarland Living Trust

About

Getting Started

Contact US

LLO Story Guide

Login

The Kay McFarland Living Trust has made it possible for you to write your story.

Please visit lastinglegacyonline.com to share what is important to you.

It's a forever gift your family and friends will always be grateful for.

the end (of this story)

How to get started

Use the QR Code below to write your Lasting Legacy Online story. Using our story prompts, you'll be asked a series of questions to help guide you to create your life story.

This is an experience for grandparents and grandchildren to do together, learning about one another while leaving their story, in their own words, for future generations. *It's the greatest gift you can give.*

It's 100% free, secure and you will not be asked to purchase anything. Thanks to Kay McFarland, Lasting Legacy Online will always remain free to everyone. Start writing your story today. Go to:

LastingLegacyOnline.com

About the **Author**

Shawn Wesner is the proud mother of three wonderful children. She works for the U.S. Department of State where she has been lucky enough to work and live in Africa and Asia. She is a certified yoga instructor who loves to write about her travel adventures.

About the **Illustrator**

Devin Wineinger loves to make unique artwork using colored pencils and markers. Her work mainly features people, plants, and animals and often incorporates steampunk or cottagecore elements. Wineinger earned a BA from Washubrn University in 2018 and one year began her own art business, Sparks & Steam. In her free time, Devin enjoys creating and wearing cosplays, reading, writing, traveling, and spending time with her family. She currently lives in Topeka, Kansas with her husband, son and two cats. To learn more, visit her website at sparksandsteam.com.

9 798991 156066